modern readers

stage 3

# The Great Invention

Eduardo Amos
Elisabeth Prescher
Ernesto Pasqualin

2nd edition

Richmond PUBLISHING

© EDUARDO AMOS, ELISABETH PRESCHER, ERNESTO PASQUALIN, 2004

**Richmond PUBLISHING**

Diretoria: *Paul Berry*
Gerência editorial: *Sandra Possas*
Coordenação de *bureau*: *Américo Jesus*
Coordenação de pesquisa iconográfica: *Ana Lúcia Soares*
Coordenação de revisão: *Estevam Vieira Lédo Jr.*
Coordenação de produção gráfica: *André Monteiro, Maria de Lourdes Rodrigues*
Coordenação de produção industrial: *Wilson Troque*

Projeto editorial: *Véra Regina A. Maselli*

Edição de texto: *Kylie Mackin*
Assistência Editorial: *Gabriela Peixoto Vilanova*
Revisão: *Denise Ceron*
Projeto gráfico de miolo e capa: *Ricardo Van Steen Comunicações e Propaganda Ltda./Oliver Fuchs*
Edição de arte: *Christiane Borin*
Ilustrações de miolo e capa: *Robson Araújo*
Foto da capa: *CID*
Pesquisa iconográfica: *Vera Lucia da Silva Barrionuevo*
Tratamento de imagens: *Fabio N. Precendo*
Diagramação: *EXATA Editoração*
Pré-impressão: *Hélio P. de Souza Filho, Marcio H. Kamoto*
Impressão e acabamento: **EGB**

---

**Dados Internacionais de Catalogação na Publicação (CIP)**
**(Câmara Brasileira do Livro, SP, Brasil)**

Amos, Eduardo
　　The great invention / Eduardo Amos, Elisabeth Prescher, Ernesto Pasqualin ; [ilustrações Robson Araújo]. — 2. ed. — São Paulo : Moderna, 2003. — (Modern readers ; stage 3)

　　1. Inglês (Ensino fundamental) I. Prescher, Elisabeth. II. Pasqualin, Ernesto. III. Araújo, Robson. IV. Título. V. Série.

03-3368                                              CDD-372.652

**Índices para catálogo sistemático:**
1. Inglês : Ensino fundamental   372.652

**ISBN 85-16-03721-5**

Reprodução proibida. Art.184 do Código Penal e Lei 9.610 de 19 de fevereiro de 1998.

Todos os direitos reservados

**RICHMOND PUBLISHING**
EDITORA MODERNA LTDA.
Rua Padre Adelino, 758 - Belenzinho
São Paulo - SP - Brasil - CEP 03303-904
Vendas e Atendimento: Tel. +55 11 2602-5510 / 0800 771 81 81
Fax +55 11 2790-1284
www.richmond.com.br
2010

Impresso no Brasil

17ª impressão — Fev/2010

# Chapter 1

"Anybody home?" shouted Neil as he knocked at the garage door.

Steve opened the door and said, "Neil! Fred! Come in."

The boys entered the garage. It was almost impossible to walk around. Cans, boxes, and tools were all over the place.

"What are you doing, Steve?" asked Fred.

"Finishing up a new invention," answered Steve. "The mechanical fingers aren't moving very well and the electronic elbow has a problem."

"Mechanical fingers? Electronic elbow? What are you working on this time?" Fred asked.

"A turnator. It turns pages for you. I think it's going to be helpful for musicians," explained Steve.

"And lazy readers," added Neil. "Fred is going to be your first customer."

Steve and Neil started laughing, but Fred didn't like the joke.

The two boys were still laughing when Fred noticed something strange in a fishbowl by the window.

"What's that in the fishbowl?" he asked.

"Another invention — a buoy for stressed fish," said Steve.

"You're really crazy, you know!" said Neil.

"Yes, but the fish are happy," replied Fred. "Look!"

"OK, you guys," said Steve. "Enough of inventions. What's new?"

"We're really worried," said Neil.

"Why? What's happening?" asked Steve.

"There's going to be a basketball game next Saturday," Fred said. "Kingsville High School is coming to play against us. Remember the last time we played them. They were really violent."

"Yes. I remember," said Steve. "Rick was hit on the head and was in hospital for two days."

"We think it's going to be even more violent this time," said Neil.

"The whole world is more violent," Steve said. "Nobody knows where things are going to end. Did you read today's paper?" he asked. "Here, look!"

## Peace Summit Threatened by Inflexibility

Powerful heads of state will be in town next week for a summit meeting on world disarmament.

The boys read the article in silence.

"Do you think there is going to be a war?" asked Neil.

"Yes, if they don't come to an agreement," answered Steve. "And it is going to be an ugly war. Perhaps the last war on our planet."

Steve's mother opened the door and said, "Sandwiches coming!" She pressed a button and a tray with sandwiches moved towards the boys.

"What's that?" asked Fred.

"Another of my inventions — a flying tray," said Steve. "Thanks, Mom."

# Chapter 2

Two days later, Steve was looking for his friends at school. He was very excited.

"Neil! Fred! We have to talk right now. It's about the basketball game next Saturday."

"What about it?" asked Neil.

"We all know it's going to be violent, right?"

"Right," they said.

"Well, I think we can do something about it. I have a plan," said Steve. He told the boys that he had invented a new gas that had the power to calm down angry people.

"OK, but what is the plan?" asked Fred.

"We fill balloons with the gas," explained Steve. "We then give them to the cheerleaders and ask them to burst the balloons during the game. The gas will do the rest."

Fred and Neil liked the plan. The three boys walked around the school to find the cheerleaders. The girls did not know the real reason for the plan. They thought it was some kind of joke and immediately agreed to help.

Neil and Fred woke up at 6:30 on Saturday morning. At 7:00, the three boys were busy working in Steve's garage. The game was going to start at 10:00.

"Steve!" said Neil after an hour working hard on their plan. "This is not going to work! The balloons burst when I blow the gas into them."

"Maybe there is too much pressure inside the balloons," said Fred. "It will never work! What now, Steve?"

"I think we have to find thicker balloons," Steve replied.

"Let's go, then! Hurry!" said Fred.

They ran to the neighborhood stores to find thicker balloons. At 9:15, they were back at the garage to test the new ones.

They had to hurry. There were fifty balloons to fill. When they finished, they rushed off to school.

"You're late, guys!" shouted one of the cheerleaders. "The game is almost over."

You could feel the tension in the air. The Kingsville team was losing, and they were getting more violent. A big fight was starting.

"Here you are, girls," Steve shouted. "Take the balloons around the gym and burst them. Hurry up! There's no time to waste!"

The cheerleaders quickly took the balloons, ran in all directions and burst them. Nobody understood what was going on.

"Stop what you are doing, girls!" somebody shouted but they didn't pay any attention.

As the gas dispersed, everybody started to calm down. The visitors lost the game, but there was no violence.

When Steve went to bed that evening, he could not sleep. He thought about the game, the violence, and the gas he had invented.

"It was the gas," he thought. "I knew it was going to work! The gas calmed everyone down."

He was lost in thought when an idea flashed through his mind. "If the gas worked on the kids, it must work on adults too," he reasoned. "There is that Peace Summit next week. Everybody is going to be tense."

He sat up in bed and reached for the telephone. He had to talk to Neil and Fred.

# Chapter 3

Mr Thompson opened his front door and found Neil, Fred and Steve on his doorstep. Mr Thompson was Neil's neighbor. He worked in the Maintenance Department at the Convention Center, the location of the Peace Summit the following week.

"Hello, boys," said Mr Thompson as he opened the door. "Quite early for a Sunday morning, isn't it?"

"Sorry for being so early, Mr Thompson, but we really need to talk to you," said Neil. "Do you have a few minutes?"

"Sure!" replied Mr Thompson. "Come on in!"

"What can I do for you, kids?" asked Mr Thompson.

They told him about the gas and what they did at the basketball game. They told him they wanted to do the same thing at the Peace Summit.

"Wait a minute!" said Mr Thompson. "Is this some crazy idea to save the world? Don't you kids realize that the Peace Summit is a very serious matter? It's not for people like you and me."

"We have to do something, Mr Thompson," insisted Steve. "The newspaper says that this is an important meeting, but the politicians are inflexible. If they can't agree, there could be a war."

"What can I do about it?" asked Mr Thompson.

"You can help us a lot," said Neil.

"But why me?" asked Mr Thompson.

"Well, first, because you work at the Convention Center," said Fred.

"And second, because we know you care," added Steve.

"Yeah. We remember that you risked your life to save those children from the fire at the shopping center last year," said Neil.

"Our plan is to spray the gas at the Convention Center during the summit," explained Steve. "The participants will be affected by the gas. They will calm down and think about peace, not war."

"You work in the Maintenance Department at the Convention Center, right?" asked Neil. "You are familiar with the building. You know your way all around the place, don't you? You can help us get into the building and reach the Conference Room."

Mr Thompson was reluctant at first. It was difficult for him to accept doing something illegal. But he was worried about the possibility of war. The boys were enthusiastic and finally convinced him to help.

"Your only access to the Conference Room is the air-conditioning system," he said. "It is full of passages, but I can make a map of the pipes for you."

"I think we are going to need maintenance uniforms and identification cards," Neil said.

"I'll take care of that," said Mr Thompson. "Don't worry."

"Good. And we are going to need walkie-talkies for communication inside the air-conditioning system," said Fred.

"And don't forget the gas!" Mr Thompson reminded the boys.

"Don't worry about that, Mr Thompson. We are going to put the gas in fire extinguishers," explained Steve.

"Well, the only thing is that we have to keep this secret. Top secret!" said Neil.

The Convention Center was busy on Wednesday morning. Reporters were everywhere. Television crews went in and out with their equipment. Limousines stopped by the main door bringing the heads of state. Security guards and police officers were everywhere.

At nine o'clock, everyone was ready to start the summit. TV floodlights went on and the chairman opened the event.

Down at the Maintenance Department, Mr Thompson was anxiously watching the closed-circuit TV.

"The meeting started twenty minutes ago and those boys are not here yet," he thought. "Security guards are all over the place. Perhaps they stopped them."

Just then, the boys ran into the room.

"Sorry we're late, Mr Thompson," said Steve panting.

"It was very hard to enter the building," added Fred.

"There are security guards at the gate," explained Neil. We had to show them our IDs and tell them a long story. Fortunately they let us in."

"Thank goodness!" said Mr Thompson. "Now let's see! Did you bring everything?"

"Sure, we have the bottles and they are filled with gas," said Fred. They took out three small metal bottles from their bags. "And we brought the walkie-talkies."

"Right, boys... we have no time to waste. Hurry!" said Mr Thompson. "Here are the maps of the pipe system. Follow the directions carefully. Now get your things and go."

"What time is it now?" asked Steve.

"Ten minutes to ten," answered Neil.

"You have only fifteen minutes to get to the Conference Room," said Mr Thompson. "I'll check you positions every five minutes over the walkie-talkie. Go, quickly!"

# Chapter 4

The way through the air-conditioning system was cold, dusty, and dark. The passages were so low that they had to crawl. Three minutes later, the walkie-talkie in Mr Thompson's hand beeped. It was Neil.

"I can't find my map! I think I lost it on the way," said the boy.

"Well, calm down and tell me where you are."

"I don't know exactly, but there is a large yellow pipe on my right," said Neil. "Shall I go on?"

"No, Neil. It's too complicated. If you go on, you'll get lost. Go back and try to find your map. It must be somewhere near you."

Two minutes later, Neil called Mr Thompson again.

"I found it, Mr Thompson. It was on the floor fifteen meters behind me. Everything is OK now."

Mr Thompson sighed in relief and thought, "Let's hope everything is really OK."

"Steve!" Mr Thompson shouted over the walkie-talkie. "Steve, give me your position."

"I think I'm doing fine," said Steve. "I am close to the air-conditioning power unit. It is very noisy and very cold here."

"OK, Steve, go on."

Mr Thompson paused for a second and looked at the clock on the wall. It was ten o'clock.

"Fred," he called over the walkie-talkie. "Can you hear me Fred?" There was no answer. He called again. "Can you hear me, Fred? What's going on?" he asked nervously. "Something is wrong," he thought.

He put his walkie-talkie on the table and went into the piping. While he was crawling inside, the walkie-talkie on the table beeped. He ran back to answer. He knew it was Fred trying to talk to him.

"Fred, can you hear me?"

"Yes, faintly," Fred said. "I think I'm lost."

"What's the matter, Fred?"

"I can't find the yellow marks on the wall. I don't know where I am. I'm scared, Mr Thompson. The plan is going to fail and it will be all my fault!"

"Look, Fred. Don't worry. Listen to me, now." Mr Thompson was sweating and spoke very slowly. "Look around. What do you see around you?"

"A green box. There is a large green metal box to my right," said Fred.

"Great! I know where you are. Go back about three meters. You'll find a fork. Take the left pipe. You'll find the marks there."

As he waited, Mr Thompson was more and more nervous. "I'm a fool," he thought. "The security guards are going to find us! I never should have..."

"OK, Mr Thompson. I found the marks. Everything is fine now."

Mr Thompson sat on the large couch in the Maintenance Department firmly holding his walkie-talkie. On the closed-circuit TV, he could see what was going on in the Conference Room. Some people gestured aggressively, others stood up and spoke angrily. They all looked very tense.

One of them walked to the microphone with a grave look on the face. He said a few words and walked back to his place. Mr Thompson got up.

"Steve! Fred! Neil!" said Mr. Thompson nervously. You have to hurry, boys. The Summit is going to finish earlier. There is no agreement. The chairman is going to read a statement in a few minutes. He's probably going to announce that the negotiations have failed. This is the end, boys. There is going to be a war. Please, hurry!"

The boys hurried. They crawled faster and faster and hurt their hands and knees. Their faces were covered with dust, but they could not cough. They had to be very silent. They knew that they couldn't fail.

"OK, Mr Thompson! I'm on target. I'm ready to go ahead," said Fred over the walkie-talkie.

"Neil!" called Mr Thompson. "Where are you?"

"Right in place, Mr Thompson," replied Neil.

"What about you, Steve?" asked Mr Thompson.

"I'm near the Conference Room," Steve answered. "But there is a grate here. It won't open. It's locked.

# Chapter 5

"Try to open it! I'm sure you'll find a way," whispered Mr Thompson over the walkie-talkie.

In the Conference Room, the chairman walked over to his secretary and picked up a sheet of paper.

"The chairman is going to the microphone now, boys. We have no more time!" said Mr Thompson.

The walkie-talkies were silent for a few seconds. Mr Thompson was terrified. The chairman walked to the microphone, took out a handkerchief and mopped his forehead. He looked around the room very slowly.

"I did it! I opened it" Steve said over the walkie-talkie. "I used my jackknife. The grate is open."

"OK, let's go, boys!" said Mr Thompson.

"Position 1 — ready," said Neil.

"Position 2 — ready," said Fred.

"Position 3 — ready," said Steve.

"OK, boys. FIRE!" said Mr Thompson.

The boys sprayed the gas, and in seconds, everyone was inhaling it.

The chairman adjusted the microphone. He looked at the document in his hands. He looked at the audience and at the TV cameras. He thought for a while and then said, "Ladies and gentlemen. I have an announcement to make. I believe we should postpone our decision. We cannot decide the future of our planet with such anger in our hearts. I suggest we take a break for lunch and finish in the afternoon."

His suggestion was unanimously approved by all those present.

Back at the Maintenance Department, the three boys and Mr Thompson celebrated the success of their plan. The boys were tired and dusty, but the gas worked.

At four o'clock that afternoon, Steve arrived home.

"Where were you all day, Steve?" his mother asked. "The school secretary called and said that you didn't go to school. You missed the news on TV. They said that the Peace Summit was a success. They are going to start a worldwide disarmament campaign. What were you doing?"

"I was working, Mom," Steve answered. Then he looked at her and smiled. "I was busy saving the world."

# KEY WORDS

The meaning of each word corresponds to its use in the context of the story (see page number 00)

**against (5)** contra
**ago (14)** atrás
**agree, agreed (8)** concordar
**agreement (6)** acordo
**all over (3)** por todo
**almost (3)** quase
**anger (23)** fúria, raiva
**angrily (20)** furiosamente, com raiva
**angry (12)** furioso, com raiva
**anybody (3)** alguém
**beep (17)** bipar
**believe (23)** acreditar
**blow (9)** soprar
**bottle (15)** garrafa
**bring, bringing (14)** trazer
**building (13)** edifício, prédio
**buoy (4)** bóia
**burst (8)** estourar
**busy (9)** ocupado
**calm down (7)** acalmar-se
**campaign (24)** campanha
**care (12)** importar-se
**carefully (15)** cuidadosamente
**chairman (14)** presidente da comissão
**check (16)** verificar
**cheerleader (8)** líder de torcida
**close (18)** próximo
**closed-circuit TV (14)** televisão em circuito fechado

**couch (20)** sofá
**could (10)** poderia
**cough (21)** tossir
**crawl (17)** engatinhar
**crew (14)** equipe
**customer (4)** cliente
**dark (17)** escuro
**doorstep (12)** porta da casa
**dusty (17)** empoeirado
**early (12)** cedo
**elbow (3)** cotovelo
**even (5)** ainda, até
**everyone (11)** todos
**everything (15)** tudo
**everywhere (14)** em todo lugar
**excited (7)** entusiasmado
**fail (18)** falhar, fracassar
**faintly (18)** baixinho
**familiar (13)** familiarizado
**faster (21)** mais rápido
**fight (10)** briga
**fill (8)** encher
**find (8)** achar
**finger (3)** dedo
**finish up, finishing up (3)** terminar
**fire extinguisher (13)** extintor de incêndio
**firmly (20)** firmemente
**fishbowl (4)** aquário
**floodlight (14)** holofote
**flying (6)** voadora

**fool** (19) bobo
**forehead** (22) testa
**forget** (13) esquecer
**fork** (19) bifurcação
**fortunately** (15) felizmente
**gate** (15) portão
**get into** (13) entrar
**get lost** (17) perder-se
**grate** (21) grade
**guys** (5) rapazes, "caras"
**gym** (10) ginásio de esportes
**handkerchief** (22) lenço
**happen, happening** (5) acontecer
**hard** (9) duro
**head** (5) cabeça
**head of state** (5) chefe de estado
**heart** (23) coração
**helpful** (4) útil
**hit** (5) bater
**hold, holding** (20) segurar
**hope** (17) ter esperança
**hurt** (21) ferir
**ID** (15) identidade
**inhale, inhaling** (23) inalar
**inside** (9) dentro
**jackknife** (22) canivete
**joke** (4) piada
**just then** (14) naquele momento
**keep** (13) manter
**knee** (21) joelho
**knock, knocked** (3) bater
**late** (10) tarde
**laugh, laughing** (4) rir
**lazy** (4) preguiçoso
**let** (15) deixar
**locked** (21) trancado
**look for, looking for** (7) procurar

**lose, losing** (10) perder
**low** (17) baixo
**main door** (14) porta principal
**matter** (12) assunto
**maybe** (9) talvez
**mind** (11) mente
**mop, mopped** (22) enxugar
**need** (12) precisar
**neighbor** (12) vizinho
**never** (9) nunca
**news** (24) noticiário
**next** (5) próxima
**nobody** (10) ninguém
**noisy** (18) barulhento
**pant, panting** (15) ofegar
**peace** (5) paz
**pick up, picked up** (22) pegar
**pipe** (13) cano
**piping** (18) encanamento
**place** (3) lugar
**postpone** (23) adiar
**powerful** (5) poderoso
**power unit** (18) unidade de força
**quickly** (10) rapidamente
**reach, reached** (11) pegar
**reader** (4) leitor
**ready** (14) pronto
**reason** (8) razão
**relief** (17) alívio
**remember** (5) lembrar-se
**right now** (7) agora mesmo
**risk, risked** (12) arriscar
**rush off, rushed off** (10) apressar-se
**save** (12) salvar
**scared** (18) assustado
**security guard** (14) segurança
**sheet** (22) folha

**should (9)** deveria
**shout, shouted (3)** gritar
**sigh, sighed (17)** suspirar
**slowly (19)** lentamente
**something (4)** algo
**somewhere (17)** em algum lugar
**spray (13)** pulverizar
**statement (20)** declaração
**still (4)** ainda
**store (10)** loja
**strange (4)** estranho
**summit meeting (5)** reunião de cúpula
**sweat, sweating (19)** suar
**terrified (22)** aterrorizado, apavorado
**thicker (9)** mais grosso
**thought (11)** pensamento
**tired (23)** cansado
**tool (3)** ferramenta
**towards (6)** em direção a
**town (5)** cidade
**tray (6)** bandeja
**try (17)** tentar
**unanimously (23)** de maneira unânime
**wake up, woke up (9)** acordar
**war (6)** guerra
**waste (10)** desperdiçar
**watch, watching (14)** observar
**while (23)** um tempo
**whisper, whispered (22)** sussurrar
**whole (5)** inteiro
**world (5)** mundo
**worldwide (24)** mundial
**worried (5)** preocupado
**wrong (18)** errado
**yet (14)** ainda

## Expressions

**all my fault (18)** tudo culpa minha
**Come on in! (12)** Entrem!
**Don't worry! (13)** Não se preocupe!
**go on! (17)** continue!
**Hurry up! (10)** Apresse-se!
**I'm on target (21)** Estou em posição
**lost in thought (11)** pensativo
**Thank goodness! (15)** Que Alívio!
**There's no time to waste! (10)** Não há tempo a perder
**They didn't pay any attention (10)** Eles não prestaram atenção
**What about it? (7)** O que é?
**What's the matter? (18)** Qual é o problema?

# ACTIVITIES

## Before Reading

**1.** Look quickly at the illustrations in the book. What kind of story do you think it is?
   a) adventure   b) romance   c) police   d) science fiction

**2.** Look at the pictures in the book. On what pages can you find...?
   _____ a walkie-talkie       _____ balloons
   _____ fire extinguishers    _____ pipes
   _____ ID                    _____ a grate

**3.** What do you think "The Great Invention" is?
   _____ a balloon             _____ a gas
   _____ a walkie-talkie       _____ a fire extinguisher

## While Reading

### Chapter 1

**4.** Read pages 3 and 4. What are Steve's two new inventions?
   a) _____
   b) _____

**5.** Describe, in your own words, what these inventions do.
   a) invention 1 is for _____
   b) invention 2 is for _____

**6.** Read page 5. Two things are going to happen. Complete the chart with the information about these two events:

|                        | Next Saturday | Next Week |
|------------------------|---------------|-----------|
| What _____ ? Where _____ ? |               |           |

**7.** Read pages 5 and 6. The boys are worried about **two** of these things. Which things? Circle them:

| | | |
|---|---|---|
| a flying tray | Steve's mother | a war |
| the gossip | violence in the world | the basketball game |

## Chapter 2

**8.** Read page 7. Why is Steve so excited?

_____
_____

**9.** On page 7, Steve says, "...I have a plan."
What do you think Steve's plan is? Discuss your ideas with a partner and take some notes:

_____
_____

**10.** Read pages 8 and 9. What is the problem with Steve's plan? Circle one of the following:

   a) The cheerleaders don't want to help.
   b) The gas is too thick.
   c) The balloons are too thin.

**11.** Read page 10 and decide whether the following sentences are True (T) or False (F).

   a) When the boys arrived at school, the game was over. _____
   b) The Kingsville team wasn't winning. _____
   c) The players were fighting. _____

**12.** Describe the cheerleaders' part in the plan.

**13.** Before you read page 11, think about what will happen next. Discuss your ideas with a friend and take notes:

**14.** Read page 11 and check your answer to 13.

**15.** Write the opposites of these words/expressions. Look for help on pages 10 and 11.

winning         _____
peaceful        _____
became tense    _____

**16.** At the end of page 11, what do you think Steve "has to talk to Neil and Fred about?"

## Chapter 3

**17.** Read pages 12 and 13 and decide if the following sentences are True (T) or False (F):

a) Mr Thompson is Steve's neighbor. _____
b) Mr Thompson doesn't agree to help the boys. _____
c) Steve thinks there is going to be a war. _____
d) Mr Thompson works at a shopping center. _____
e) The boys can enter the Conference Room through the air-conditioning system. _____

**18.** The boys need some items for their plan. Circle the items which are mentioned on page 13.

| | | |
|---|---|---|
| a map | fire extinguishers | uniforms |
| identification cards | walkie-talkies | gas |
| a car | radios | flashlights |

**19.** Look at the pictures on pages 14 and 15. Find these things in the picture and number them.

1. security guards
2. a walkie-talkie
3. ID

**20.** Read page 15. At the entrance to the building, the boys had a problem. Why?

### Chapter 4

**21.** Read pages 16 to 21. Who does these things? Write (F) Fred, (S) Steve or (N) Neil.

_____ loses his map.

_____ can't find the yellow marks on the wall.

_____ finds a locked grate.

### Chapter 5

**22.** Read pages 22 and 23 and put these events in the right order.

a) The chairman postponed the decision about the future of the planet.
b) The boys sprayed the gas into the Conference Room.
c) The boys celebrated the success of their plan.
d) The participants approved the chairman's decision.
e) Steve opened the grate with a jackknife.

**23.** Read page 24. Imagine you are a reporter. Write a short news story that summarizes what Steve's mother saw on TV.

```
PEACE SUMMIT A SUCCESS
```

## After Reading (Optional Activities)

**24.** Discuss these statements. Do you agree or disagree?

"Mr Thompson was wrong to help the boys. He worked in the Maintenance Department and he did something illegal."

## 25. Mini-projects

a) In the story, the boys find an invention for peace — "a gas that calms people down." In groups, think of some ways to reduce violence in:

your neighborhood/town
OR
your country
OR
your world

b) Discover an organization/campaign in your community whose objective is to reduce violence or promote peace.

c) Think of an invention for another problem in your neighborhood, city or country. Describe it to your classmates. Possible problems:

> pollution      traffic
> crime          health